ALEXANDER HAMILTON
(1755 – 1804)

QUOTATIONS

OF

Alexander Hamilton

APPLEWOOD BOOKS
Carlisle, Massachusetts

Alexander Hamilton

ALEXANDER HAMILTON, American statesman and Founding Father, was born in Charlestown, on the leeward islands of the British West Indies on January 11 in either 1755 or 1757. He and his older brother, James Jr., were born out of wedlock to Rachel Faucette and James A. Hamilton. The discrepancies in birthdate arise from Hamilton's reporting 1757 as his birthdate upon arrival in North America. However, court records from his mother's death support his birth as 1755. He arrived in the colonies in October 1772 and completed grammar school in New Jersey. Hamilton entered King's College (today's Columbia University) in New York City in the autumn of 1773 and graduated in May 1774. He played a major role in the American Revolution, joining a militia in 1775, then becoming a senior aide to George Washington during the war. Hamilton was then elected to the Congress of the Confederation for New York, the first form of government in the new nation. After a brief tenure of four months he started a law practice. Hamilton married Elizabeth Schuyler December 14, 1780, and fathered eight children. He led the call for a national government to form a new constitution. Hamilton was elected a delegate to the constitutional convention in Philadelphia in 1787. He wrote the majority of *The Federalist*

Papers, which served as supporting documents in ratifying the U.S. Constitution. He was selected the first secretary of the treasury in 1789, under President George Washington, and served in that role for five years. Founder of the Federalist Party, he believed in a strong federal government in support of commerce, manufacturing, agriculture, and a national military. He advocated funding states and national debts and creating a tariff system, and he established the first national bank. The author of the Jay Treaty, he strengthened the trade ties with Great Britain, averting further war. The treaty led to the two-party system in the United States. In 1795 Hamilton returned to practicing law and business activities in New York City. In 1797, Hamilton admitted to an extramarital affair and being blackmailed by his mistress and her husband. Hamilton's longtime conflict with Aaron Burr stemmed back to 1791, when Burr defeated Hamilton's father-in-law, Philip Schuyler, for a U.S. Senate seat. In the election of 1800, Hamilton supported Thomas Jefferson when he and Aaron Burr tied in the electoral college, relegating Burr to vice-president. Hamilton campaigned hard for Burr's opponent in seeking the office of governor of New York in 1804. The hostilities between the two men came to a head when Burr mortally shot Alexander Hamilton in Weehawken, New Jersey on July 11, 1804, and he died the following day in Greenwich Village, New York City.

QUOTATIONS

OF

Alexander Hamilton

To confess my weakness, Ned, my Ambition is prevalent that I contemn the grov'ling and condition of a Clerk or the like, to which my Fortune &c. condemns me and would willingly risk my life, tho' not my Character to exalt my Station. Im confident, Ned that my Youth excludes me from any hopes of immediate Preferment nor do I desire it, but I mean to prepare the way for futurity. I'm no Philosopher you see and may be jus[t]ly said to Build Castles in the Air. My Folly makes me ashamd and beg youll Conceal it, yet Neddy we have seen such Schemes successful when the Projector is Constant. I shall Conclude saying I wish there was a War.

– Letter to Edward Stevens in St. Croix regarding his ambition, November 11, 1769

Our distressed helpless condition taught us humility and a contempt of ourselves.— The horrors of the night—the prospect of an immediate cruel death—or, as one may say, of being crushed by the Almighty in his anger—filled us with terror. . . . Our imagination represented him as an incensed master, executing vengeance on the crimes of his servants.—The father and benefactor were forgot, and in that view, a consciousness of our guilt filled us with despair.

– Letter to his father in the colonies about experiencing a hurricane on St. Croix, September 6, 1772

A Hamilton

There is a certain enthusiasm in liberty, that makes human nature rise above itself, in acts of bravery and heroism.

– "The Farmer Refuted," February 23, 1775

A Hamilton

A fondness for power is implanted, in most men, and it is natural to abuse it, when acquired.

– "The Farmer Refuted," February 23, 1775

The sacred rights of mankind are not to be rummaged for, among old parchments, or musty records. They are written, as with a sun beam, in the whole volume of human nature, by the hand of the divinity itself; and can never be erased or obscured by mortal power.

– "The Farmer Refuted," February 23, 1775

If Congress have not yet left Philadelphia, they ought to do it immediately without fail, for the enemy have the means of throwing a party this night into the city. I just now crossed the valley-ford, in doing which a party of the enemy came down & fired upon us in the boat by which means I lost my horse.

– Letter to John Hancock after encountering British troops near the city, September 18, 1777

It is a maxim with some great military judges, that with sensible officers soldiers can hardly be too stupid; and on this principle it is thought that the Russians would make the best troops in the world, if they were under other officers than their own.

– Letter to John Jay, March 14, 1779

*Y*ou should not have taken advantage of my sensibility to steal into my affection without my consent.

– Letter to Colonel John Laurens, who left General Washington's military to return to his home in South Carolina, April 1779

*I*t is very certain that the military Career in this country offers too few inducements; and it is equally certain that my present Station in the Army cannot very long continue under the plan, which seems to govern.

– As Inspector General of the Army, in a letter to Captain George Izzard on not depending on a military career, February 27, 1780

I have told you, and I told you truly that I love you too much. You engross my thoughts too intirely to allow me to think of any thing else . . . . 'Tis a pretty story indeed that I am to be thus monopolized, by a little nut-brown maid like yo— and from a statesman and a soldier metamorphosed into a puny lover. I believe in my soul you are an inchantress.

– Letter to Elizabeth Schuyler two months before their marriage, October 5, 1780

$\mathcal{S}$ometime last fall when I spoke to your Excellency about going to the Southward, I explained to you candidly my feelings with respect to military reputation, and how much it was my object to act a conspicuous part in some enterprise that might perhaps raise my character as a soldier above mediocrity. . . .

– Letter to George Washington requesting a field command,
  November 22, 1780

A Hamilton

$\mathcal{A}$ national debt, if it is not excessive, will be to us a national blessing; it will be a powerful cement of our Union.

– Letter to Robert Morris, April 30, 1781

A Hamilton

$\mathcal{Y}$ou cannot imagine how entirely domestic I am growing. I lose all taste for the pursuits of ambition, I sigh for nothing but the company of my wife and my baby. The ties of duty alone or imagined duty keep me from renouncing public life altogether.

– Letter to Richard Kidder Meade, former aide-de-camp for General
  George Washington, March 1782

*U*nless we can overcome this narrow disposition and learn to estimate measures, by their general tendency, we shall never be a great or a happy people, if we remain a people at all.
– "The Continentalist," No. V, April 18, 1782

I have thought it my duty to exhibit things as they are, not as they ought to be.
– Letter to Robert Morris, August 13, 1782

*T*he weak side of a republican government is the danger of foreign influence.
– Debate at the Constitutional Convention, June 18, 1787

I believe the British government forms the best model the world ever produced, and such has been its progress in the minds of the many, that this truth gradually gains ground. . . . All communities divide themselves into the few and the many. The first are the rich and well born, the other the mass of the people. . . . The people are turbulent and changing; they seldom judge or determine right. Give therefore to the first class a distinct, permanent share in the government. They will check the unsteadiness of the second, and as they cannot receive any advantage by a change, they therefore will ever maintain good government.

– Farrand's *Records of the Federal Convention of 1787*, v. 1, p. 299, June 19, 1787

A Hamilton

One great error is that we suppose mankind more honest than they are.

– Debate at the Constitutional Convention, June 22, 1787

A Hamilton

Vigor of government is essential to the security of liberty. . . .

– *The Federalist Papers*, Federalist No. 1, October 27, 1787

A Hamilton

Were there not even these inducements to moderation, nothing could be more ill judged than that intolerant spirit which has at all times characterized political parties.

– *The Federalist Papers*, Federalist No. 1, October 27, 1787

*I*t has been frequently remarked that it seems
to have been reserved to the people of this
country, by their conduct and example, to decide
the important question, whether societies of
men are really capable or not of establishing
good government from reflection and choice,
or whether they are forever destined to depend
for their political constitutions on accident
and force.

– *The Federalist Papers*, Federalist No. 1, October 27, 1787

*I*n politics, as in religion, it is equally absurd
to aim at making proselytes by fire and sword.
Heresies in either can rarely be cured by
persecution.

– *The Federalist Papers*, Federalist No. 1, October 27, 1787

*T*he violent destruction of life and property
incident to war, . . . will compel nations the most
attached to liberty to resort for repose and
security to institutions which have a tendency to
destroy their civil and political rights. To be more
safe, they at length become willing to run the risk
of being less free.

– *The Federalist Papers*, Federalist No. 8, November 20, 1787

The rights of neutrality will only be respected, when they are defended by an adequate power. A nation, despicable by its weakness, forfeits even the privilege of being neutral.

– *The Federalist Papers*, Federalist No. 11, November 24, 1787

A Hamilton

Why has government been instituted at all? Because the passions of men will not conform to the dictates of reason and justice, without constraint.

– *The Federalist Papers*, Federalist No. 15, December 1, 1787

A Hamilton

When the sword is once drawn, the passions of men observe no bounds of moderation.

– *The Federalist Papers*, Federalist No. 16, December 4, 1787

A Hamilton

I seldom write to a lady without fancying the relation of lover and mistress. It has a very inspiring effect.

– Letter to sister-in-law Angelica Church, December 6, 1787

*E*xperience is the oracle of truth; and where its responses are unequivocal, they ought to be conclusive and sacred.

– *The Federalist Papers*, Federalist No. 20, December 11, 1787

*T*he natural cure for an ill-administration, in a popular or representative constitution, is a change of men.

– *The Federalist Papers*, Federalist No. 21, December 12, 1787

*I*t is a singular advantage of taxes on articles of consumption that they contain in their own nature a security against excess.

– *The Federalist Papers*, Federalist No. 21, December 12, 1787

*T*he fabric of American Empire ought to rest on the solid basis of THE CONSENT OF THE PEOPLE.

– *The Federalist Papers*, Federalist No. 22, December 14, 1787

*L*aws are a dead letter without the courts to expound and define their true meaning and operation.
– *The Federalist Papers*, Federalist No. 22, December 14, 1787

*T*he means ought to be proportioned to the end; the persons from whose agency the attainment of any end is expected ought to possess the means by which it is to be attained.
– *The Federalist Papers*, Federalist No. 23, December 18, 1787

*I*t is a truth, which the experience of ages has attested, that the people are always most in danger when the means of injuring their rights are in the possession of those of whom they entertain the least suspicion.
– *The Federalist Papers*, Federalist No. 25, December 21, 1787

*W*ar, like most other things, is a science to be acquired and perfected by diligence, by perserverance, by time, and by practice.
– *The Federalist Papers*, Federalist No. 25, December 21, 1787

The citizens of America have too much discernment to be argued into anarchy.
– *The Federalist Papers*, Federalist No. 26, December 22, 1787

Man is very much a creature of habit. A thing that rarely strikes his senses will generally have but little influence upon his mind.
– *The Federalist Papers*, Federalist No. 27, December 25, 1787

In the usual progress of things, the necessities of a nation in every stage of its existence will be found at least equal to its resources.
– *The Federalist Papers*, Federalist No. 30, December 28, 1787

The obscurity is more often in the passions and prejudices of the reasoner than in the subject.
– *The Federalist Papers*, Federalist No. 31, January 1, 1787

The propriety of a law, in a constitutional light, must always be determined by the nature of the powers upon which it is founded.
– *The Federalist Papers*, Federalist No. 33, January 2, 1788

*T*o model our political system upon speculations of lasting tranquility, is to calculate on the weaker springs of the human character.
– *The Federalist Papers*, Federalist No. 34, January 5, 1788

A Hamilton

*N*ecessity, especially in politics, often occasions false hopes, false reasonings and a system of measures, correspondently erroneous.
– *The Federalist Papers*, Federalist No. 35, January 5, 1788

A Hamilton

*C*ommon interest may always be reckoned upon as the surest bond of sympathy.
– *The Federalist Papers*, Federalist No. 35, January 5, 1788

A Hamilton

*J*ustice is the end of government. It is the end of civil society. It ever has been, and ever will be, pursued, until it be obtained, or until liberty be lost in the pursuit.
– *The Federalist Papers*, Federalist No. 51, February 6, 1788

*L*aw is defined to be a rule of action; but how can that be a rule, which is little known, and less fixed?
– *The Federalist Papers*, Federalist No. 62, February 27, 1788

*I*f mankind were to resolve to agree in no institution of government, until every part of it had been adjusted to the most exact standard of perfection, society would soon become a general scene of anarchy, and the world a desert.
– *The Federalist Papers*, Federalist No. 65, March 7, 1788

A feeble executive implies a feeble execution of the government. A feeble execution is but another phrase for a bad execution; and a government ill executed, whatever may be its theory, must be, in practice, a bad government.
– *The Federalist Papers*, Federalist No. 70, March 15, 1788

*M*en often oppose a thing, merely because they have had no agency in planning it, or because it may have been planned by those whom they dislike. But if they have been consulted, and have happened to disapprove, opposition then becomes . . . . an indispensable duty of self-love.

– *The Federalist Papers*, Federalist No. 70, March 15, 1788

*T*hat experience is the parent of wisdom is an adage the truth of which is recognized by the wisest as well as the simplest of mankind.

– *The Federalist Papers*, Federalist No. 72, March 19, 1788

*T*he injury, which may possibly be done by defeating a few good laws, will be amply compensated by the advantage of preventing a number of bad ones.

– *The Federalist Papers*, Federalist No. 73, March 21, 1788

*A*nd it proves, in the last place, that liberty can have nothing to fear from the judiciary alone, but would have everything to fear from its union with either of the other departments.
– *The Federalist Papers*, Federalist No. 78, May 28, 1788

*N*o Legislative act, therefore, contrary to the Constitution, can be valid. To deny this, would be to affirm, that the deputy is greater than his principal; that the servant is above his master; that the Representatives of the People are superior to the People themselves;
– *The Federalist Papers*, Federalist No. 78, May 28, 1788

*T*he Courts must declare the sense of the law; and if they should be disposed to exercise will instead of judgement; the consequences would be the substitution of their pleasure for that of the legislative body.
– *The Federalist Papers*, Federalist No. 78, May 28, 1788

A power over a man's subsistence amounts to a power over his will.
– *The Federalist Papers*, Federalist No. 79, May 28, 1788

*I*t has been observed that a pure democracy if it were practicable would be the most perfect government. Experience has proved that no position is more false than this. The ancient democracies in which the people themselves deliberated never possessed one good feature of government. Their very character was tyranny; their figure deformity.

– Speech in New York urging ratification of the U.S. Constitution, June 21, 1788

A Hamilton

*T*he truth is . . . the Constitution is itself, in every rational sense, and to every useful purpose, A BILL OF RIGHTS.

– *The Federalist Papers*, Federalist No. 84, July 16, 1788

A Hamilton

*C*onstitutions should consist only of general provisions; the reason is that they must necessarily be permanent, and that they cannot calculate for the possible change of things.

– Elliot's *Debates*, volume 2, p. 364, July 28, 1788

I never expect to see a perfect work from imperfect man.

– *The Federalist Papers*, Federalist No. 85, August 13, 1788

*A*nd as, on the one hand, the necessity for borrowing in particular emergencies cannot be doubted, so, on the other, it is equally evident that, to be able to borrow upon good terms, it is essential that the credit of a nation should be well established.

– "Report on Public Credit," January 9, 1790

*T*he spontaneous transition to new pursuits, in a community long habituated to different ones, may be expected to be attended with proportionably greater difficulty.

– "Report on Manufactures," December 5, 1791

*I*t was not 'till the last session that I became unequivocally convinced of the following truth: That Mr. Madison cooperating with Mr. Jefferson is at the head of a faction decidedly hostile to me and my administration, and actuated by views in my judgment subversive of the principles of good government and dangerous to the union, peace and happiness of the Country.

– Letter to Edward Carrington, May 26, 1792

*M*r. Jefferson has hitherto been distinguished as the quiet, modest, retiring philosopher—as the plain simple unambitious republican. He shall not now for the first time be regarded as the intriguing incendiary—the aspiring, turbulent competitor.

– "Catallus, Number III," *Gazette of the United States*, September 29, 1792

*T*he impression is uniform—that your declining [to run again for President] would be to be deplored as the greatest evil, that could befall the country at the present juncture, and as critically hazardous to your own reputation. . . . If you continue in office nothing materially mischievous is to be apprehended—if you quit much is to be dreaded.

– Letter to President George Washington encouraging him to run for a second term, August 3, 1792

*U*nder every form of government, rulers are only trustees for the happiness and interest of their nation, and cannot, consistently with their trust, follow the suggestions of kindness or humanity towards others, to the prejudice of their constituents.

– Notation in the margin of *Gazette of the United States* and not in the draft of "Pacificus No. IV," July 10, 1793

*I*t is long since I have learnt to hold popular opinion of no value.

– Letter to President George Washington from western Pennsylvania after subduing the Whiskey Rebellion, November 11, 1794

I consider the cause of good government as having been put to an issue and the verdict against it.

– Letter to Rufus King regarding proposed amendments to a finance bill intended to retire the debt in thirty years, February 21, 1795

*T*he laws of certain states . . . give an ownership in the service of Negroes as personal property. . . . But being men, by the laws of God and nature, they were capable of acquiring liberty—and when the captor in war . . . thought fit to give them liberty, the gift was not only valid, but irrevocable.

– "Philo Camillus No. 2" essay, 1795

A Hamilton

The passions of a revolution are apt to hurry even good men into excesses.

– "Philo Camillus No. 3" essay, August 12, 1795

A Hamilton

The nation which can prefer disgrace to danger is prepared for a master, and deserves one.

– Letter to *The Daily Advertiser*, February 21, 1797

A Hamilton

The charge against me is a connection with one James Reynolds for purposes of improper pecuniary speculation. My real crime is an amorous connection with his wife for a considerable time, with his privity and connivance, if not originally brought on by a combination between the husband and wife with the design to extort money from me. . . .

– Observations of documents in "The History of the United States for the Year 1796, No. V & VI," regarding his affair with Maria Reynolds, August 25, 1797

I am more and more the fool of affection and friendship. In a little time I shall not be able to stir from the sides of my family & friends.
– Letter to sister-in-law Angelica Church, January 22, 1800

*N*othing has given me so much chagrin as the Intelligence that the Federal party were thinking seriously of supporting Mr. Burr for president. I should consider the execution of the plan as devoting the country and signing their own death warrant.
– Letter to friend James McHenry, January 4, 1801

*L*et it be remembered that Mr. Burr has never appeared solicitous for fame, and that great Ambition unchecked by principle, or the love of Glory, is an unruly Tyrant which never can keep long in a course which good men will approve.
– Letter to James A. Bayard characterizing Aaron Burr, January 16, 1801

*M*ine is an odd destiny. Perhaps no man in the U[nited] States has sacrificed or done more for the present Constitution than myself. And contrary to all my anticipations of its fate, as you know from the very beginning, I am still labouring to prop the frail and worthless fabric. Yet I have the murmurs of its friends no less than the curses of its foes for my rewards. What can I do better than withdraw from the scene? Every day proves to me more and more that this American world was not made for me.

– Letter to Gouverneur Morris of New York, January 27, 1802

*M*en are rather reasoning than reasonable animals, for the most part governed by the impulse of passion.

– Letter to James A. Bayard, member of U.S. House of Representatives (Delaware), April 16–21, 1802

A garden, you know, is a very usual refuge of a disappointed politician. Accordingly, I have purchased a few acres about nine miles from town, have built a house, and am cultivating a garden.

– Letter to Charles Cotesworth Pinckney of the Federalist Party, December 29, 1802

*A*rm yourself with resignation. We live in a world full of evil. In the later period of life, misfortunes seem to thicken round us and our duty and our peace both require that we should accustom ourselves to meet disasters with Christian fortitude.

– Letter to wife, Elizabeth Hamilton, March 17, 1803

*I*t is the Press which has corrupted our political morals — and it is to the Press we must look for the means of our political regeneration.

– Brief before New York Supreme Court in *People vs. Croswell*, February 13, 1804

*I*f it had been possible for me to have avoided the interview, my love for you and my precious children would have been alone a decisive motive. But it was not possible, without sacrifices which would have rendered me unworthy of your esteem. I need not tell you of the pangs I feel, from the idea of quitting you and exposing you to the anguish which I know you would feel. Nor could I dwell on the topic lest it should unman me. . . . Adieu best of wives and best of women. Embrace all my darling Children for me.

– Letter for delivery to wife, Elizabeth, if he is killed in duel with Aaron Burr; July 4, 1804

I have resolved, if our interview is conducted in the usual manner, and it pleases God to give me the opportunity, to reserve and throw away my first fire, and I have thoughts even of reserving my second fire.

– Letter the night before duel with Aaron Burr, July 10, 1804

*L*astly, I shall hazard much, and can possibly gain nothing by the issue of the interview. But it was, as I conceive, impossible for me to avoid it. There were intrinsick difficulties in the thing, and artificial embarrassments, from the manner of proceeding on the part of Col Burr.

– Statement on the impending duel with Aaron Burr, written June 28–July 10, 1804

I will here express but one sentiment, which is, that Dismemberment of our Empire will be a clear sacrifice of great positive advantages, without any counterballancing good; administering no relief to our real Disease; which is Democracy, the poison of which by a subdivision will only be the more concentered in each part, and consequently the more virulent.

– Letter to Theodore Sedgwick the night before the duel with Aaron Burr, July 10, 1804

*T*he Scruples of a Christian have determined me to expose my own life to any extent rather than subject my self to the guilt of taking the life of another. This must increase my hazards & redoubles my pangs for you. But you had rather I should die innocent than live guilty. Heaven can preserve me and I humbly hope will but in the contrary event, I charge you to remember that you are a Christian. God's Will be done. The will of a merciful God must be good. Once more Adieu My Darling darling Wife.

– Second letter to wife, Elizabeth, the night before his duel with Aaron Burr, July 10, 1804

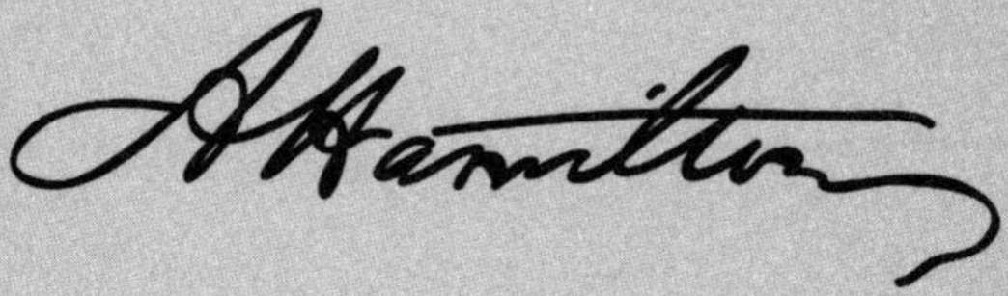
A Hamilton